IT HAD TO BE TOLD!™

BE TOLD!

PUBLISHING

I want to tell you a story...
ONE THAT I STILL CAN'T BELIEVE!™

This book is dedicated to Steve Bartman, a fan
who loved his team, the Chicago Cubs.

I want to tell you a story, one that I still can't believe.
It's the story of the Chicago Cubs of 2016.

...but before we begin, I want to revisit the past, back to 1908, when the Cubs won their last.

"Let the good times roll," all of
Chicago thought,
"the Cubs will be great forever!"
All the tickets were bought.

...then something strange happened in the year 1945,
people at the game couldn't believe their eyes.
At Game Four of the World Series, a man's goat wanted a seat,
but the goat smelled so bad, it brought fans to their feet.

"Don't let that smelly goat in!" the people did shout.
So the two were stopped at the gate and booted right out!
"You will never win again!" the man proclaimed aloud,
and thus "The Curse of the Billy Goat" fell over the crowd.

Chicago was leading that Series, two games to one,

but darn if the Cubs didn't lose it. It was really no fun.

For years, then decades, the curse seemed to hold true,
as the Cubs kept losing, it was all they could do.
Season after season, the "Loveable Losers" seemed destined to fall.
"Someday the Cubs will be in the World Series!"
became Harry Caray's signing off call.

...that was until one bunch gave the city hope,
with a new batch of players, a GM and a coach.

So the fans put on their jerseys, their hats and their gloves,
and headed down to the ball park that they all know and love.

WRIGLEY FIELD
HOME OF
CHICAGO CUBS
GO CUBS GO! 2016

WELCOME TO THE FRIENDLY CONFINES
WELCO NDLY CONFINES
WELC NDLY CONFINES
WELCOME TO THE FRIENDLY CONFI
GO CUBS!
CUBS
CUBS

I WANNA
PARTY
LIKE IT'S
1908
WORLD TITLE

Wrigley Field is the place, the home of this team,
the Chicago Cubs of 2016!

The season is new, the city's all here,
generations of families all ready to cheer!
"Go, Cubs, Go!" blasts over the speakers,
as the Cubs-faithful quickly fill up the bleachers.

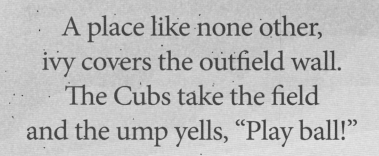

A place like none other,
ivy covers the outfield wall.
The Cubs take the field
and the ump yells, "Play ball!"

They were ready to go, this young, scrappy team,
thanks to a master plan by GM Theo Epstein.

The coach was Joe Maddon, a real positive guy,
he told his Cubs to believe in themselves and to reach for the sky!

Fowler lead the way, he was as fast as they come,
he would steal every base, man could he run!

Rizzo and Bryant had power
and could both flash their glove.

They even signed Chapman,
who threw 100 and above!

Baez and Russell were young, but wow, could they play!

Ross and Zobrist brought experience
to show them the way.

When Arrieta and Lester took the mound, it all seemed to work.
Plus, Hendricks and Lackey had guys chasing pitches in dirt.

Even the team from St. Louis
stood no chance at all.
The Cubs reached 103 wins,
the best team in baseball!

They raised the "W" high above the city each night,
that big white flag flying over Wrigleyville - what a glorious sight.

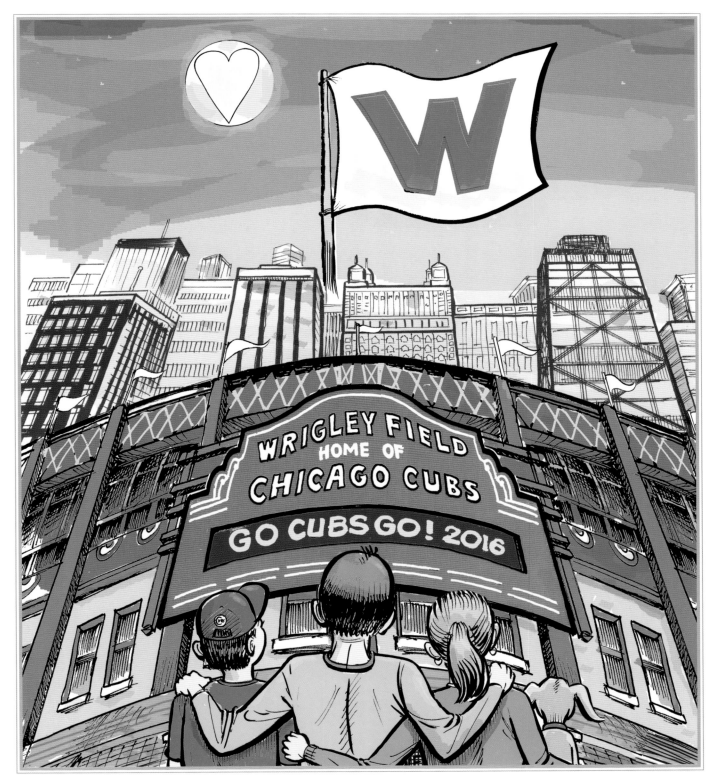

They won the Central Division, and all our hearts too,
then on to the Playoffs to see what they could do.

They took care of the Giants from San Francisco Bay

then handled the Dodgers who hail from LA.

On to the World Series where Cleveland would wait,
facing a drought of their own, the matchup seemed to be fate.

The big hitter, Schwarber, worked hard to make it back from the DL, but even with his boost, things didn't start well.

After four games they trailed and fans all started to worry,
own three games to one, the "Curse of the Billy Goat" was back in a hurry.

...but this was a new century's team, not the Cubs of old.
Two big wins and they were one win away from the gold.

Game Seven in Cleveland was one of the best of all time, there was even a rain delay, fans were losing their minds!

Heyward rounded up his mates and told them to believe.
He said, "This is our team, our city, our dream!"

The game went into extra innings as Zobrist stepped to the plate,
a hit here and the pain would be over - no longer would Chicago wait.

A crack of the bat
brought the fans to their feet;
the go-ahead run crossed the plate,
bringing joy to
West Addison Street.

The bottom of the inning finally
went the Cubs' way,
a third "OUT!" with a smile would
be the World Series final play.

The curse was broken! The "Lovable Losers" ceased to be,
the Chicago Cubs had won the World Series, four games to three!

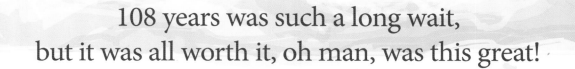

108 years was such a long wait,
but it was all worth it, oh man, was this great!

That smelly billy goat would curse them no more,
thanks to a 10th inning win, eight to seven the score!

It was finally over, a feeling that they couldn't believe,
the Cubs were World Champions, the year - 2016!

From the Author

Growing up, I was all about sports - football, soccer, baseball, you name it. If it wasn't sports related, I wasn't interested. My love for sports is a passion that has shaped my entire life. I am fortunate to play soccer for a living, but it's bigger than that. My most cherished childhood memories are centered around watching a big game; my relationship with my wife sparked by a mutual love for Penn State football, and my passion for Tampa Bay sports keeps me close to home, even though we've moved all over the country. I owe so much of my life to sports.

The idea to tell these stories came about after the birth of my daughter, Remy. I wanted to create a vehicle that I could share my love of sports with her, in a way that would hopefully build a bond we'd share forever. Reading together provides a way for parents and their children to share in special moments, but I want these stories to do even more. I want to reach the kids like me, the ones more likely to grab a ball than a book. It is so important for a growing mind to fall in love with reading and I hope these stories can bridge a love for sports with a newfound passion for reading.

— Jeffrey Attinella

About the Illustrator

Mike Pascale (mikepascale.com) is a storyboardist, artist, writer, comic book creator (Bru-Hed), and former award-winning ad agency copywriter/senior art director. Between storyboarding films and drawing this children's book, he writes and draws the world's longest-running football webcomic, "Game BUZZ!," every week at gamebuzzcomic.com. A Californian born and raised in metro Detroit, he had a lot to learn about the Cubs, and found all of it fascinating, frustrating, fun, funny, interesting and incredible. He only hopes he was able to entertain Cubs fans and do justice to their team's titanic tale—and that we don't wait another century for their next well-deserved WS win! GO CUBBIES!

...a few of our other books